Life *in* *Verses*

BETTY DAVIS

authorHOUSE®

AuthorHouse™
1663 Liberty Drive
Bloomington, IN 47403
www.authorhouse.com
Phone: 1 (800) 839-8640

Published by AuthorHouse 10/03/2019

ISBN: 978-1-7283-2944-4 (sc)
ISBN: 978-1-7283-2943-7 (e)

Library of Congress Control Number: 2019915344

Print information available on the last page.

Any people depicted in stock imagery provided by Getty Images are models, and such images are being used for illustrative purposes only. Certain stock imagery © Getty Images.

This book is printed on acid-free paper.

Contents

II. Religion

III. Romance

IV. Philosophies

Acknowledgement

Those I want to recognize who had some impact in my life which inspired me to write this book is my mother Janie Davis, my father Jeff Davis, Grandmother Mattie Davis, Dr. C. O Henry, my first grade teacher Goldie Pugh. Her words were "Go ahead you can do it", my late husband Rev. Benjamin F. Davis, Rev. Rufus Johnson who encouraged me after I first began. Major General John Phillips who advised me at some point. My children Joseph Davis, Mathais Davis, Leslie Davis. With my grandchildren in mind I made my final decision to get this book published. I give gratitude to Bill Goree a dear friend who inspired me to continue writing after a long break.

Preface

I began putting my feeling on paper because I was shy about speaking to others about my feelings. I hope someone somewhere will get some joy and comfort as I do from my writings. The life I have lived, the things I have seen in life combined are a fact. I was not sure as to what I would do about my dreams. I decided not to attend college I spent most of my spare time in the library, later I did an on the job training program in Dental Assisting. I have lived my life always putting God first. I have often thought of visiting every State in the USA, I have traveled the majority. Designing clothes, creative writing, doing art work Advertising signs for small businesses was a joy doing. My dreams were being fulfilled. My desire was to marry a man who believed in God. I later married the late Rev. Benjamin F. Davis. At this moment my dreams are all being fulfilled.

LIFE IN VERSES

Contents of this publication were organized,
developed and edited

By

Betty Jo Davis
Frankston, Texas
2019

Typed by

Billy J. Goree
Mathais C. Davis
Betty Jo Davis

Computer Graphics
Images, Typing

Betty J. Davis
Mathais C Davis
Billy J. Goree

Preface by
Betty Jo Davis

Cover
Betty J Davis

I. Life

A City Called Life

There is the city called life,
There is three streets in this city.

The street of Happiness,
The street of Heartache,
The street In-between

The street of Happiness
The broadest
The highest, and one path.

The street of Heartache
too low too rough for any man to survive
A street of destruction.

The street In-between
where men really live,
One where every man walks
in heartache, happiness, and
all things to be found in life.

If we are on the street of Happiness,
Let us try and keep life a beautiful city.
If we are on the Street of Heartache,
let us not run into destruction,
take the right detour out.

If we are in-between, let us realize
that we cannot live in life without
happiness or heartache.
Life itself is happiness and heartache.

To live in life, we live the way
we prefer, our destiny, we have no say.

The street of Happiness
a path over life,
The street of Heartache.
A tunnel under Life.
The street In-between,
consist of both, Happiness and Heartaches
run right through the heart of life.

After Death

Death makes me feel like a child waiting out a storm.
An underground storm room,
fighting off flies and crawling insects

Death taught me,
Never have or show pity
Just trust in God

Shock, feels like it never happened.
Yet, death itself is proof

Fear, why am I afraid
What am I afraid of?
Death is one on one.

Loneliness, Death why did you take away from my Life?
Sudden tears, from what fountain did you flow?

Guilt, Why are you here?
Who was those that was here?

They are the ones that are gone.
They are the ones, I loved.

Why did I have to stay?
Why did you have to go?

Death has made its visit.
Depression, loneliness, guilt,
Life, show me some peace!

Guilt will come, guilt will fade away.
Depression, Loneliness will someday take a break.
Peace will come again, that will be a better day.

As long as I stay and others go,
Guilt will come, depression, loneliness, will
return another sad day.
That's life way.

America the Great and Beautiful

America is a great and fortunate country.
Country that often criticized.
Sure this country has a great quantity.
Of crime, poverty, prejudices.

We criticize America for giving foreign aids
we complain about taxes.
Why don't we take a better look at our country.
Take a good look at other countries, life is never all good.

There has been complaints about America getting into foreign affairs.
Let us look at it this way, perhaps America is so great and fortunate
due to the aid America is giving others.

In many foreign countries, there are those who don't believe in God.
We have those who don't believe in God,
yet more people believe in and worship God in America than any country.

Wouldn't you think that God has something to do with
America being so great and fortunate.

Here

Here I came, here I've lived.
Here, I've found, here, I've lost.
Here, I've lied, here I've been truthful.
Here, I've gone wrong, from here, I'm going right.

Because

Because I didn't am not.
Because I should have and didn't
I'm not what I ought have been.
Whether it's not what I want to be.

Death

Death is after that life I've lived
And will live no more.
Death is a thing
I some time dread to know.
Death is what I fear,
And why, I don't know,
Why should I?
After death what is there
for me to know?

Definition of Life

Addition is birth,
Multiplication is more life
Division is separation,
Subtraction is death.

Happiness and Heartaches

Happiness is like a bird flying through fresh air,
The farther it flies, the farther it can fly.
Heartache is like a burred insect.
No matter how he digs,
There is always something in his path.

Success

The early train was crowded,
I refused to board it, didn't want to fight the crowd

I caught the late train, a very light crowd.
If I had caught the early train,

I would have made it in time.
Today success would have been mine.

Stayed Too Long

Go away loneliness,
I need happiness, yes I need happiness.

Come on happiness,
I am tired of loneliness, yes tired of loneliness

Go away loneliness,
I need you happiness.

Where are you happiness?
I know where you are loneliness.

You are staying away too long happiness.
I see you happiness, good by loneliness.

So happy, happiness.
So long, loneliness.

I Am Not Ashamed

The Lord made me black
I am not ashamed.
His reasons, I will not question.

I've been mistreated,
yes, I've been called dumb.
I've been beaten, kicked,

I've been called dirty, been lynched
many times my life's been taken.

Yes, though I've been abused,
I will not be shamed.
I will not let my past stand in the path of my future.

I will strive to do and be the best
not for my self alone, for my Race.
Surely God will see, I've done my job.

Surely I will stand as tall, and be
treated as an individual who is qualified.

All the days that will follow,
I will fight to keep the respect that
I have gained for my race, for the Human race.

I Cant Stop Living

I cannot stop living, Life is so beautiful,
A few dark shadows, that's hardly my concern

I can't stop living, I have dreams,
Dreams that need to become a reality.
A reality that will be mine to church.

I can't stop living, there is success, the sweet aroma of success.

I can't stop living, I need to feel happiness, to deal with heartache.

I can't stop living, I've yet to find myself
a self that lost something within itself.

I can't stop living, life needs fulfilling,
for that fulfillment, I haven't given
myself a chance.

I can't stop living cause I'm not yet dead.

If The World Was Mine

If I could make the world over, I would make everybody
that's referred to as nobody, a somebody.
Everybody that's referred to as somebody
would not be a somebody compared with that
so called nobody that I made a somebody,
with that somebody not a somebody compared with
that nobody I made a somebody,
I would have made a world of equal bodies.

I have lived, I Have Learned

I have lived, I have learned,
I have seen right and wrong,
I have experienced right and wrong.

I have lived, I have learned
I have seen hell, I have lived through hell
I have seen happiness, I have lived in happiness.

I have lived, I have learned,
I will live, I will learn.

Life

Full of additions, divisions, and subtractions
A child out here, in this world wondering without a care.

A grown up, all full of knowledge
caught in a prison of love, hate, doubt, and responsibilities.

All concluding in one figure
Hard, cold, strangest and deep.

Live God like your reward will be eternal life,

Happiness multiplied by happiness.

Life from Every Angle

I've explored life from every angle
Dived into life, to its deepest depths.

Climbed the highest peak in life
To the highest ever seen.

Fallen as far as fate would allow
Rose as high as fate would allow.

I've explored life from every angle
Driven life's longest mile.

Yet, nowhere have I been successful
in finding complete happiness.

What does it Take

It takes a man and a woman to began a life.

It takes money to support a life, love and
guidance to make life worthy.

It takes many pennies to keep life going,
pennies that profits many pennies in return.

It takes death to end a life,
money out of respect, to rest in style.

My Mother My Father

When I entered this city called life,
As I walk the streets of happiness,
they were there to share every glorious moment, My Mother, my Father.

When I crossed too fast at the cross roads in life they were there,
My mother, my father.

When life knocked me to my knee,
they were there,
My Mother, My Father.

When I lost the best thing within myself,
They were there My Mother, My Father
Their teachings were there to help correct this thing My Mother, My Father.

My Journey to Success

The early train was full,
I refused to catch it,
Cause I hate fighting the crowd.

I caught the late train
The crowd was light,
I knew the journey would be right.

Just before we entered the city
of the young and restless,
The train Detoured.
Ahead, there was miles of confusion.

We soon arrived in the city of matrimony,
There was a long hot and many storms,
many years of compromises.

We arrived in the city of child bearing
there was a track derailed.
Went through, the city of Responsibilities

The train was loosing time.
Success was yet a long distance away.

As we entered into no finances,
my train jumped track, another delay.

Time was lost on repair, and re-board
I said to my self, forget this.

I thought I would never reach success,
At that moment, I recalled my mothers advice.

You cannot reach Success if you don't work own your delays.

Life has its own delays.

Father on up the track,
I went to the front of the train,
up ahead success was in sight.

I looked up to Heaven, I prayed
"God speed up this train,
I need to make it on time,
I need success to be mine.

No, I did not catch the Early Train the right time,
But I thank God I made it in time.

Today, Success is Mine.

My Walk

I walked down a street in life, many curves and detours.
I detoured instead of going straight, a terrible mistake.
At the main intersection, I crossed too fast
I was hit with the facts of life, I payed with a great price.
The impact was Quite destructive, yet, it left me without a lane.
Being on optimist, destruction is not my aim.

Cares I've lost

The cares that concern me yesterday,
I lost them somewhere before today,
Lost among the trouble I had,
between yesterday and today.

Somewhere between today and tomorrow,
I will find those cares I lost,
Those lost, between yesterday and today.

Until I find what I had yesterday,
Those things lost sometime before today,
I will just be contented with
what fate allow me to keep today

Dont let Me Pass Success

Don't let me pass success by today,
I need it now and tomorrow.

Don't let me over look success today,
Tomorrow I need to be on my way.

Don't let me walk by success today,
I did yesterday, I'm still sorry today.

I need success to keep me going,
Keep going or lose the joy of having a complete life.

A life of success, multiplied by success.
Success plus Happiness.

Life and Death

Once you are born,
At that moment life exist.
After you are born,
Death is a sure thing.

We own many material things in life
Our lives are just an untimely loan from God.

God promised us eternal life
Add all godly things to your life.
Subtract all ungodly things
Eternal life will be happiness plus.

Enjoying God's Creation

Today I am cruising peacefully
A place I thought I would never be.

Quietly enjoying God's beautiful waters,
Sitting here watching the waves that will
never flow the same again.

God's great creation, one out of mercy,
that is a mystery to see.

We dream we plan we live.
Our dreams are sometimes fulfilled,
other times not.

Our families a joyful time to share with another.
Our children, our grands and great grands
fills our heart with joy.
Our retirements, where do we go from there?

God blessed, us again, he allows us to reach back,
enjoy old friends.
A pleasure we didn't have time for before.

This is where my life is.
I cannot ask for a better time
than where I am today.

Remember Yesterday

Today we love without love,
When we say good by, no heart is broken.
Remember yesterday, when we loved with love.

Today we love without love,
We live in unsatisfied love affairs.
I remember yesterday when we lived with love.

Today we seem to have forgotten,
Its better to have loved with love.
Sad not to to love at all.

Life without love is not the beautiful life we once lived.
If it could only be beautiful.
Remember yesterday, when we loved and lived in love?

Where am I?

Hot and sweaty, mean and muddy,
Where am I?
Southeast Asia Soldier,

Where do you want to be?
Home my Superior, far in the West.
Home where I can live in peace, where fear will cease.

Fear, courage, however I exist, I must fight on.
Hate, contentment, how ever I feel,
I cannot quite now.

Far from home, lonely and sad,
Where did you say I am my Superior?
Southeast Asia Soldier, where did you say you want to be?

Far, far in the West,
Home in America with family.
Home where I can be my best.

A Self That Lost the Best

A self that taught honesty,
A self that build its life by honesty.

A life lived in honesty, been so foolish,
So foolish to think it could live with itself,
After being unfaithful to itself.

An incident that caused a change to its pledge to honesty,
A self that lost the proudest thing within itself.
A need to correct this dishonesty, more would be lost than gained.

Because of that, this self will have to live with itself,
A self that may never again be proud of itself.

Keep Me an Optimist

Keep me an Optimist, I dream of dreams that come true.
Keep me an Optimist, everything's beginning to be alright

Keep me an Optimist, life was alright yesterday,
I knew it would be, the day before.

Keep me an Optimist, life is ok today,
Just like it was yesterday.

Keep me an Optimist, I need life to be ok tomorrow.
Fate promised me yesterday, and kept its promise today

Keep me an Optimist, I was yesterday I am today.
Surely tomorrow will be no difference from yesterday or today

Never so Proud

I could say hello this morning
I did say good night
I'm glad about it.

I sat up, I get out of my bed
I lived today as fully as I could
I'm glad about it.

I did every thing I could today
I finished the things I could yesterday
Don't tell me, I'm not glad about it.

I believe that tomorrow,
I cannot look back, and be unhappy
I'm glad about it.

Nor am I a Welcomed Guest

I am not a stranger in any land
nor will I ever be

I am not a stranger anywhere
nor am I a welcome guest.

I am an unwanted visitor
A visitor without an invitation.

I am not a stranger anywhere
Nor am I a welcomed guest.

I've visited the young, visited the elders
I'm not a stranger to any one nor am I a welcome guest.

I'm a visitor to all kind.
Sometime I'm not expected.

Everyone knows me
I'm not a stranger to anyone, nor am I a welcomed guest.

I'm never a welcomed guest,
Sometime I'll not a stranger.

Yet, everyone knows me, I'm death.

The Black Boy

Years ago the Civil War was fought,
the Black Boy fought.

World War I was fought,
it of my knowledge that the Black Boy fought there.

The war was over, life was tough for him
He was mistreated, lynched killed.

World War II was fought, the Black Boy did his part,
returned home, things were still bad for him, a few changes were made.

The Korean War was fought, the Black Boy fought there,
Life was the same when he returned.

During the years that followed, the Black Boy found life better for himself.
He still had hell making a decent place for himself in this Caucasian World.

The Black man is complaining about Black fighting in Vietnam,
the White Boy is fighting for his people, his country.

If the Black Boy does not fight,
who is going to fight for us Blacks who are complaining.

The White Boy think enough of his people to help keep the communist away.
If the communist take control, Blacks won't be an exception.

Many wars have been fought since the Civil War,
If Uncle Sam kept the Black out of the services,
Black lips would be stuck out about that.

Somewhere in the future will be the end of the Black mans misfortunes.
Let us keep fighting, our misfortunes will become good fortunes.

Slowly Uphill

There is this town called I won't.
It's just down the hill from never will.

Just around the corner is I can't.
It's a place where I'm not sure of myself.

On my way out of I can't
I am sure I'll pass around the quicksands of I might.

There is a way out,
I am sure I'm right.

The next stop, I make will be tough,
The first big step up the hill.

This Day

Sunrise and morning Sun,
After that, the morning Bright.

As I make this Journey,
I know not what lies ahead.

This Journey, I must make,
Whether a failure or success.

Where as I believe success is so for away,
So near it could be.

The Creation of Me

With dad,
With mom.

All together,
Now alone.

Dad gave me,
Mom grew me.

Life experiences taught me,
Now I'm out here trying the best
to live with me.

There is an Occasion

There is an occasion for everything in life.
I have the time, I have the occasion.
I will make my life the occasion.

The Way of Life

Yesterday we were all there,
yes all together, sisters and brothers,
cousins and friends.

We climbed the trees, we hiked in the woods,
fought the wasps, caught the bees.

Played in the mud, crawled over the leaves,
walked the barn tops.

Did everything until we were told to stop.
Today, we are apart, sisters here and there,
brothers over yonder.

Cousins no telling where, friends scattered
caught in the slums, sleeping in the cold, God only knows how many been
bumped.

Very Little Do I Know

Very little do I know about hate,
Every I know about love.

Very little can I tell about hate,
A lot I can tell about love.

Very little do I hate,
A lot do I need to love love.

So much I see of hate,
So much I need to love.

Very little have I to hate,
For I am determine to live with love.

Tomorrow

Who was one to say there is no tomorrow?
He who was here yesterday and today,
has seen tomorrow.

Yesterday, today was tomorrow,
today has been tomorrow

Tomorrow, today will be yesterday
tomorrow, tomorrow will be today.

The day after tomorrow,
tomorrow will be yesterday.

Every yesterday has been tomorrow, so has today.
Who was one to say, there is no tomorrow.

Yesterday Today Tomorrow

Yesterday, my lover walked away,
Left me in a world, sad and lonely.
Today, I'm sitting here with tears in my eyes,
Wondering why, how could my lover walk away.

Tomorrow I will find another lover, a true love.
To you who heart could be broken.
Broken because of that lover who won't stay true

Yesterday is gone, forget it, today is here live with it.
Tomorrow will surely to come,
Come with happiness and love to stay.

Yesterday is gone, we have finished with that time.
Today is here, let us do the things in life,
We didn't take time to do yesterday.

II. Religion

A Prayer To Myself

God give me strength to do and continue to do thy will.
Keep me in this good peace of mind
Let not the trouble of the world depress me.
Let me remember, I have everything to be thankful for.
Help me to accept life as it come.

A Prayer To our Young Men in Vietnam

Our young men who are in Vietnam.
God be with them for one day,
they will be safe at home,
one day, they will be safe
as we are today this we pray.
Let this day be soon, keep them safe
Lead them safely away from death,
Please help them safely home.
We know you have the power.
We continue to pray on,
Prey that our young men
will make it safely on home.

Are You Ready

I want to be ready when my Jesus comes.
When Jesus comes there's no need to put your dentures in.
Jesus will accept you, toothless,
just be ready, keep your life in order.

If you are taking a shower,
there is no shame in going naked just be ready.
Keep your life in order.

There will be no need to comb your hair.
Jesus will accept your nappy head or tangled hair.
No one will see your toothless mouth,
no one will see your naked body,
No one will see your nappy or tangled hair.
Heaven will be so beautiful, everything and everyone.

I'm In Love

I'm in love with the man, Jesus Christ.
Do you know him?

I couldn't help falling in love with this man.
He's always been so good to me.

When I'm sad, he wipes away my tears.
He guides me in every decision I make.

When I'm in pain, He heals my body.

When I get depressed from life's hand me outs.
He sends the Holy Spirit to comfort me.

He died for our sins, rose on the third day,
How can we not love this man.

Jesus Christ, Son of God, King of Kings,
Lord of Lords.

Definition of Sin

Sin is dark, Sin is ugly
Who wants to live in darkness?
Who wants to be ugly?

Follow Jesus,
There will be no walking in darkness.
Jesus is the light of life.

That light is bright and beautiful,
That light will show us how to be free,
Free from sin,
That light is Jesus.

Satan

When I was young, living a careless life.
I turned my back on Christ.

Satan took me through the wilderness
I experienced the sins of the world.

Somewhere In the wilderness
I heard of King Jesus, Interesting man.

I followed Jesus, did his will
Satan has no chance, he had to let me go

Although Satan was pushed aside,
He is still trying to get back in.

Help Mother

Lord help mother to keep the faith,
Faith that I may grow to be worthy as her child.

Give her strength to teach me right from wrong,
Give her courage to protect me from
the wicked things in this world.

Give her wisdom to learn the new
ways of this changing world,
Help her do these things so that she may teach me,
so that I may teach mine, and so on.

Dear Dad,

They just don't know, but I do
you are one of a kind dad,
You were there when I needed you.
Thank God you were there when I didn't need you.

Yes, you are one of a kind.
I am sorry I never told you so,
But now you know.
My special way of caring is thanking God you are my Dad.
I'm sorry for the ones who can never say
I'm grateful to you dad.

God is the Answer

I had problems, I called my friends,
they were busy, promised to help
some other time.

I had problems, I called my next door neighbor
I had to look farther.

I've lived my life doing for others,
according to God's will.
Yet, when I called others, I got no response.

I called on God, he was there in no time.

Mother's Day

Dear Mother,

I am writing this letter because there are times,
I don't say what I feel.
Mother's day is a day for you.
I need to thank you mother for the time you spent
giving me love and teaching me what love is about.
I need to thank you for giving me a chance to be educated,
so that I might use my knowledge for a worthy purpose.
I need to ask you forgiveness for the times
I didn't listen, the times I thought I knew best.
And most of all thanks for teaching me,
there is a true and living God.
I am a mother, I will teach
love and care for my child as you did for me.
One day, I will be a proud mother when my child stands and tells me
thank you mother.

Sincerely
Your Child, Betty

Lord Help Me

Lord help me!
I have come to a time in my life sometime,
I cannot face tomorrow.

Lord help me!
I have come to a time in my life,
I am happy today has brought no more sorrow.

Lord help me!
I want to once more feel enthusiastic about life.

Lord help me!
I need courage, I need faith, I need you Lord.

My Cousin Willie

God blessed us with joy,
A son, brother, father, nephew, cousin, and a friend.

Treasured memories are left with us.
The pat you gave us on our head,

The joy we felt, when you entertained us with humor,
We will smile each time we think of you.

Willie you did well with your fellow man,
Your showed love and much joy.

Love is the key to eternal life.
It should b a joy in every man life to show love.

We realize you just took a mandatory vacation.
We will be waiting for that day, when Jesus returns.

We will all be together there, when the gates of Heaven sings open,
We can all just walk right on in.

Vernell

Yesterday we were all together,
sisters and brothers, cousins and friends.
Mom and dad were there to guide us.
As we grew older, we each went our own way
Today I'm happy that we grew up in a God fearing home.
Many times I think about during the years of your illness,
you never met a stranger.
When you left us, you also left many friends
Today, I can see the happy look on your face,
the times we visited you.
I can also feel the big hugs you gave us.
On behalf of our sisters and brother,
these memories we will always keep in our hearts.

Betty

To Kelvin

A precious brother is gone, your voice is silent,
but your memory is loud and happy.

Thursday, we sisters and brothers were altogether,
mom, dad, grandmother, cousins and friends.

Friday, you left us,
There is a vacancy in our house,
one That will never be filled.

You kept us filled with laughter and joy.

Our thoughts today are that, you are safe,
wrapped in the arms of Jesus.

At times when we find ourselves missing you,
we still hear your laughter, see your smile.

Your smile will be our smile,
Your laughter will be our laughter.

Your memory will be with us every second,
every minute, every hour, everyday, every week,
every month, year after year.

Aunt Amie

A precious mother is gone, your voice is silent,
But your memory is loud and happy.
Tuesday, we were all together, sister, brothers,
mothers, fathers, cousins and friends.
Wednesday, you left us, there is a vacancy in our home
and that will never be filled.
You kept us filled with love and joy.
Our thoughts today are that you are safe,
warped in the arms of Jesus.
At times when we find ourselves missing you.
We still hear your laughter and see your smiles.
Your smile will be our smile, your laughter will be
our laughter. Your memory will be with us every
second, every minute, every hour, everyday, every week,
every month, year after year.

Versie

Yesterday, when we spoke with you said, "I am alright"
Today, you are with God, we know that you are alright.

After we grew up, you never stop being a sister,
you became more.
You were always a friend,

You were a mother with lots of good advice, and guidance.
We shared, had lots of good laughs

You were a teacher, taught us with God in our life,
We had the key to a good like.

You will always be here with us through the
results of your caring,
God knew you needed rest, when he
whispered peace be yours.

Mama Jane's Girls

Mama Jane taught her girls to respect.
taught them to respect all.

Respect all, regardless to
who or what color.

Who are Mama Janes Girls, Edna, Mattie, Vernell, Janie
and Betty.
These are Mama Jane's Girls.

Time for marriage, God blessed Mama Jane's Girls.
God blessed her girls with God fearing husbands.

Husbands who knew their roll in marriage.
Husbands who took care of their family.

Today Mama Jane's Girls' husband are all with God.
Mama Jane's Grands or the greatest there are.

Mama Jane, your girls are all okay.
God has one, Grand children has taken charge.
God continues to bless Mama Jane's Girls and all.

III. Romance

A Great Lover

Every day a lover is born.
The greatest lover am I.

I am the one your love is for,
Here is the reason why.

My love is sweet, my love is swell,
My love is kind oh so swell.

I can make you smile, make you cry,
Make you want me and wonder why.

Make you want to live. Make you want to cry.
Believe me it ain't no lie.

Although I say this, it is not because I am a fool,
It's just the feeling of a lover who is cool.

A Message

Man of my satisfactions
Doctor of teeth in profession.

A sweet, sweet connection,
O how I love making that connection.

So cruel is fate, Afraid am I to put up my stakes.
But what the hell, might as well,
Life is only for a spell.

Never believed in love at first sight, this time am I right?
Just setting there in that chair,
Just knowing he was there.

That was enough although it was much tuff.
Had to play it cool not room for a little fool.

Now the coast is clear,
Cannot understand why I fear?

Like to know where I stand,
Would like to try for one of those gold bands.

Bill

Remember that day, long ago, that sad day,
When I was setting out side, looking down that lonely road.

Remember that battle between happiness and loneliness,
That battle, where loneliness, defeated happiness?

Remember I ask someone to help happiness,
When I thought my life would be no more.

When you came into my life,
You charged in with affection, kindness and concerns.

Today loneliness lay defeated, Happiness got up, gain the victory.
Loneliness will never again defeat happiness, like long ago.

With happiness, my life will never be the same as before.
The only sting in my heart is the fact that,

Three others made it so destiny hinders us from complete happiness,
I do understand.
You make me feel that feeling, that God created for a woman to feel for
her man.

Friendship

Friendship is my next door neighbor.
I rather have friendship my lover.

I have been accepted in his quarters as a friend,
Friendship refuses to accept me as a lover.

If friendship was my lover,
His quarters quarters would be a life filled with happiness.

If I could be friendship lover,
The definition of happiness would be changed.

If friendship would be my lover,
I would not allow fate to deal any marked cards.

He Made Me Free

I am free,
He taught me to Love again.

Yes to love again,
He stayed by my side.

The fear is gone away,
The trust is here to stay.

Yes he made me free again,
Free to be free.

He made me love again,
Taught me to trust again.

Yes, see all the things I have missed,
Although he will never be mine,
I will always love him.

He made me free again,
Yes, free to be free

I Will Love You

I need someone to love me.
Do you need someone to love you?

If there has been no one to love you,
like There has been no one to love me.
I will love you.

If you ever need someone, like I need someone,
If there is no one, here is someone, I need you.

If you need someone to hold you,
Like I need someone to hold me.

Here is someone, I love you.
I need you, I am someone.

Love Is

Yes, love is hell,
Love is until you are with your one and only.

Love will make you do what you thought you would never do.
Love will make you cry, when you are not in your lover arm,
There is a reason why.

Yes love is some time hell, yet its swell,
Love is that way, I assure you.

I know cause, I've been in it.
Believe me, you don't want to ge out of it.

Love Lingers

You were here just a second,
Went away, said you would be back in a minute

Was gone for hours,
Come back, stayed all day.

I want you to listern
Cause here is what I have to say

I am walking out next week,
I'll see that you have enough love to keep.

Be gone for months,
During my absence, You'll have years to regret.

You may hate me for decades,
But your love won't fade.

In generations to come.
I hope you will understand.

Love will be here for centuries,
True love will linger evidently.

My Man

My man, I need a whole lot of a man.
I don't need many.

He just got to have plenty,
Plenty good loving, lot of good sense

My man, he got to be cool.
I don't want no fool.

My man, I want his love, want it strong.
Man don't treat me wrong.

I want his love early morning, middle day.
Late, late in the midnight.

Without my man's love, nothing is right.
If any of you men is qualified, see to it that I get notified.

The 100ᵗʰ Psalm O Love

Make known to me that I am yours,
Serve me with happiness.

Come before my presents with love,
Let me know that, it is me you love.

I am yours, enter into my heart with love,
Be thankful for my love,

My heart is open to you.
Hope your heart is open to me forever.

The Psalm of Love

You are my love, I will not love another,
You taught me to love as one should.

You lead me up the path of happiness.
Your tenderness comfort me.

Yes you are my love, I will love you forever.
As long as you are with me I will love you.

I place my love right here before you,
I need your love to over flow in return.

I know my love will continue,
All the days we are together,
We will dwell in each other love forever.

Untie This Bond

I realize I could be too late, please try for me,
Try now to get away?

I had you once, I couldn't believe in you, I loved you careless,
Give me a life time to love you again.

Please try for me? Try now to get away.
I will do all I can to right my wrong.

Tell her I need you, Tell her I love you.
Tell her, there is a man somewhere for her, make her understand.

If your heart tells you to stay, don't keep me hanging on.
Just make your life with her, a happy.

My life would be peaceful, my life would be an ecstasy,
Just untie this bond and let me go.

Why

My love is all gone, my dear one.
My love and trust all gone.

Why my love one, must we give all we got?
Why my love one, must love be so complicated?

What happens to that love and trust, we hold so dear?
Where my love, where must I go from here?

Why Cant We

Some time I wonder if he ever loved me.
I have loved him for years.
A few blissful times and many tears.

Every thing he does and say is,
I love you, I want you, I will always need you.
Yet I don't know what will become of this thing I have for you.

I love his, I need him,
Why can't I live the remain of my life with him?
I will forever love him.

I cannot think of, giving or sharing this love.
I love him, I need him.
Why can't I live the remain of my life with him?

If I could forget, I could love another,
If I could stop remembering,
I would not need to forget.

I try to make myself believe, I don't love him,
My thoughts always concluding at, I love him,
Why can't I live the remaining of my life with him?

How Can I

I am so sad, I don't know what to do,
If I could only forget you, My life wouldn't be so blue.
If you would only allow me to love you.

What must I do, just to forget you.
I realize things are over, yet I just cannot seem to forget.
I am so hopeless in love with you.
Why don't you do the things you use to do?

I love you so, if I could only forget,
What would I have to remember?

Early Yesterday

Early yesterday, everything was alright,
Right now, this day I don't know what to say.

Yet looking ahead, somewhere tomorrow,
I am sure my life will be as rewarding as yesterday,
and not as hopeless as today.

Walking Right In

I am walking back into your life,
You can't keep me out, I have got my ticket in my hand.

I am walking back into your life,
Don't try to turn me around, don't try to keep me away.

I am walking in today,
My life will be fill with joy, love, and happiness.

Tomorrow you will be in my life,
There to stay.

You

You, you darling, smashed hope,
You interfered with my dreams.

You took my heart, took my love,
Never though you would.

I thought I had your love, had hope, happiness,
I knew I had everything.

When I look down by my side,
I see a reminder,
A reminder you will never take away.

Go help Happiness

I was setting out side one day,
A beautiful day, but quite still.
I looked up the road, you will never guess what I saw.

There were two figures traveling down the road fighting all the way.
I set and waited until the battle was ended,
One figure lay still, the other came forward.

I couldn't believe what I saw,
It was loneliness, standing strong.

I ran inside, it did no good.
Loneliness caught me at the door.

If anyone should hear of this battle,
This battle so lone ago, please go help Happiness,
or my life will be no more.

I Want To Be Free

I want to be free,
Want to be free to love,
Yes free to love again.

I want to be free from fear,
If only the fear would go away,
If only the trust would come to stay.

I want to be free, to be free,
Just want to be free.

I want to be free again,
I want to trust again.
I want to kiss, to miss.

I want to love, and to be loved.
I just want to be free, just let me be free,
Free to be free

Ben

Ben, our time together was short, our love was long and deep.
When you asked me to marry you, your next words were "I'll take care of
you". Now that you are with God our Father and Jesus Christ our Savior,
our time of taking care of each is over. God is there, taking care of you.
God is here taking care of me, Where ever we are King Jesus is there,
we are still linked together. My job now is, living to get back with you.
When I get there we can enjoy our heavenly rewards together. You always
said "It's not so bad dying, if you die in Christ", I saw you die in Christ, I
will continue to live in Christ, that is the only way back to each other. I
saw you working for Christ until you could not make another step. What
I saw, God saw too.

The last words you said to me is,
"I love you too Betty"

I Love You Ben.

IV. Philosophies

Dreams come true when one stops dreaming.

To understand the Bible, read not with your
eyes alone, but put your heart into it.

The most destructive thing in life is fear.
The most rewarding thing courage.

It takes a mind to dream,
It takes work, faith, courage and money
To support a dream

While loneliness was keeping me a prisoner
Happiness decided to take a stroll

Unhappiness is often pleased with
The victory of loneliness

Every Man is a prisoner to
some responsibility

The things I fear in life are the ones
I come across more often

To be successful, don't ask yourself, can I?
Tell yourself, I can.

We take medicine to heal our wounds an kill our
pains. Reading the Bible will heal troubled souls
and destroy a depressed mind

We say we are free, no individual is completely free.
We are prisoners to life's ups and downs.

Life can not be rewind nor can it be fast forward.
Life can only be in play mode until, life ends.
Life is some what like a recipe, you'll have to
pack the right ingredient into it, to make it good.

We often use the expression, Wait broke the wagon
down, What is it that lifts the wagon?

A grape vine is filled with sour grapes, Conversations
are sometimes likewise. Where danger is present so is God.

One cannot live on this earth alone, yet, sometimes it is
Hell trying to live with others.
In every adult, there is a little child.

Life is some what like a vehicle on rough road,
getting into rut after rut.

Love has hidden respect has found its place,
Once where there was love, now its only respect.

When I stop resenting the things, I dislike to do,
They became easier to do.

I looked miles for love and found it within inches.

Many times life has knocked me to my knees but,
never has pride refused to lift me up.

Yesterday I was standing here waiting for tomorrow.
Today, I'm sitting here wondering why.

We wait for life to began. We wait for the good times to happen.
Yet, death needs no waiter. Death takes what it wants, at anytime.

A sales person goes from door to door leaves, unhappy when the
sale is not done. Death goes from life to life, and leaves
Contented, cause his job is well done

Death is the Captain in my life.
When death presents itself.
We all must lay down and obey.

Loneliness is an Isolation, Living is an Insulation. Life is a beauty
that is painted, loveliness of living.

Living can be made successful by ignoring fate.

Hate has many hinders. Love has a surface that no hate can
penetrate. Undecided, is like knowing what to do, but not
ready to do anything about it.

Average is like not being to little, or too large,
Just being what others can accept.

Should Death pass me by again, I will live everyday with special care.
Creativeness, is a special gift from God.

Fear is a prison within our minds. Our courage is locked in this prison, with in our minds.

Each day I live, I will the next day with only
the good memories.

Sometimes I am sad. Sometimes I'm happy.
Who am I? I am life.

Death walks behind us, along life's way. Only once
does it get ahead, and step in its foot steps

Enough is more then I had, and everything,
I've always needed.

Ignorance is not knowing as much as one should.
Yet knowing as little as one cares to know.

Where ever I go, what ever I do. I will always leave something
behind. If I have a need to return. I will be welcome with wide
open arms.

Why take that from someone else, When I can make it for myself.

Once an Individual gets on the wrong path, Life is like a road being
repaired. You detour or run into construction.

Why be like everybody else, be a special body of your own,
Somebody and not everybody" Will want to be like you.

God forgives and let live. Surly man can forgive and
live contented.

Some heartaches are made. Happiness
is earned.

Dreams are sweet, Sometime so sweet, one become
Afraid of reality. A dream not fulfilled is just a sweet image.

An individual is only indispensable to his own being.

I don't remember one saying do it right, If I heard, I don't remember
Yet I'm doing it right.

Waiting time is one job,
no individual is capable of mastering.

If I could live a perfect life, I would want the exiting world
To live that life.

Take me as I am, love me as I am. I'll be as you want me to be
And more.

Meantime is until I do after I know,
I need to do. Until is before I have done or,
Whenever I do.

Maturity is a fully grown person who has no further to grow
Mentality

Memories make many bearable Today and Tomorrows
Many of us spend a lifetime trying to figure a way to
make life perfect.

Ones conscious has the key to lock out any Temptation
But sometimes chose not to.

A dreamer lives a lifetime planning his life. A fool spends a life over
coated with deceit.

A wise man live a sweet life of knowledge, candy coated with good
judgment. Optimist looks up a train track where there is
no possibilities of a denial.

A pessimist tends took look over his shoulders, thinking that evil is
always waiting for an ambush.

Being successful does not mean being one of the best. Kindness out of
duty is good for receiver. Kindness from the heart is good for the
receiver and rewarding for the giver.

Nothing can not be defined because nothing is
none existent. Life is a check written by God,
for an unlimited amount.

Love fades, but leaves some unknown tie that it is there forever. A friend
has the easiest chance to deceive, he's in. Any enemy is out, he has to get in
that is to do what a friend can.

Our earthly life is like a checking account, A checking account you deposit, you withdraw, you use, its gone. Life you live, you enjoy life, life is over, You or clone

Ignorance is a nut that can be screwed on any bolt.

Disappointment is like a railroad track, a railroad track runs through, every town, Disappointment comes through every individual life.

Be careful of who you ask advice. You may receive unworthy advice and lot of publication.

Bitterness in life has imprison human minds in webs of evilness.

Sorrow from death, is healed by the length of time.

One must have a purpose in life, in order to live Satisfactory.

The difference in life and Dreams, Dreams can be fulfilled. Life is a chance to Fulfill.

Advice can be a help or a hinder. If all good Dreams were fulfilled, Life for every individual would be perfect.

An individual who has done well in his profession is like a new recipe, that has been used and come out a goodie.

Yesterday is gone, forget it. Today is here live with it. Tomorrow could be, let's us do what, we should have done Yesterday and didn't do Today.

While you are loving your friends and watching your enemies,
You should be learning to love your enemies and watching
your friends.

Ladies, profession on the feet bring tears of joy.
Profession on the back bring tears of sorrow

Life is a formula of love, hate happiness, and sadness
The solution, is always clearer with a promise of eternal life.

Giving a wise man advice is like giving a live man life

A fool plans his path as he go along
A wise man has his path long planned

If you don't make the highest in profession, be the biggest in
Character, and best you can in both.

Cause I did!!
I'm am now the Boss that I wouldn't be, If hadn't done
What I was suppose to do

How could death be so proud?
What has it done, except make me sad?

Fast!! is a short way to go, a long distance..
Can't is when one could but, never does
Carelessness is a lazy way to care..

Caskets are retirement places for the dead
Cozy dreamers has at least one dream that comes true.

Pray to God daily to help you to continue thy will.
We live, smile and do wrong today, but somewhere along,
Tomorrow's way, There is a day to pass, a day called Payday.

One man's wrong doings, is another man's hard time
Dreams can be sweet, Life is sweet and sour.
Life is sometime hard because we make that way.
Decide what you want to be, then live to be it.

Don't worry about the discomforts of your love ones.
Every man has his ups and downs
Strive for what you want, on the road to success,
Don't do any tail stepping.

Keep between you and your fellow man, though in a way
He will understand you are not during any tailing behind.

Don't do things against others, because of what others did to you
Yet let no one walk on your tail.
Say what you believe but, never make the other fellow
Feel as though his beliefs are not considered.

An individual never knows the catacombs of life, life is full of chances.
If an individual goes through prepared, when the downfall begins life
won't be so rugged.

Destroy from yourself conscious of all petty fears that has
been stored due to past mistakes

The average individual today think that whatever one man will do,
Every man will, Whether right or wrong.

Happiness is the result of good deeds. Heartaches are the result of life.

Live as close to God as possible with realization that no Man lives
without sin. We are all sinners.

The son of God suffered, God love us, so that he let him suffer for us.
Surely he love us enough to relieve us from our suffering.

When the Conscious began to talk, whatever the temptation is, let it
Find its resting place outside.

Wherever the bible is nesting. Rest your eyes within its contents.

Ugly is a face that beauty cannot hide.

Failure is success sliding down hill.
Success is I plan, I did I am.

Prosper is when one work employees into many dollars.

Nobody is somebody who has never done anything,
Isn't during anything, nor ever intended to.

Quality is the best I have within, regardless
To what I look like outwardly.

Zippers are fasteners, like love between a Woman and a Man.
They both serve the same purpose, to interlock.

X rays shows your physical photographs
One though and action shows your mental photographs.

Yonder is Further then, That which,
You can see, and beyond that which
You can not see!

Yield to the warnings in life, and there will be
fewer fatal crashes.

Violate the laws in life and you pay you
Cannot set for yourself.

Violence is a furious way to be Forceful.

Reverse my life and start anew, What would I do
But the same thing again.

After one loses a love, Its like laying down his hunting
Guns until the next season!

If I had the power to make myself over,
I would make me happiness.

If I was the fastest being on earth, I would catch it
I would make it I had I have.

Unhappiness is the deterioration
Of all emotions. Happiness an explosion of all emotions.

If I had the price to buy fate I would write a check for
Eternal Happiness

Unite me with happiness Pack us with love
Seal us like forever.

Unhappiness, is a non-contented happiness

Forgiveness is a willing way not to resent!!

Fortunes are success that has not been tampered with by fate, or
Failure that has been ruled by fate.

Opportunity is a precious gift that life offers us all,
Whether we accept it or not.

Friendship is a trust that fate cannot destroy.
Faith is hope that will be!

One who lives a good life, should not be afraid of Death.
Death is a path we proceed through on our journey to eternal Happiness!

God comes out of us through our conscious.

To know that you are doing wrong is knowing God
Extend a kind word, it won't take from you,
It will give to needed Human being.

Beneath the person I seem to be,
The person I am lies silently with me

Every Man's life is a story
That's never been told.

Bumming is a worthless way to be a beggar.

Busy is a fast way to keep occupied.

Brute is a beast of a way to be a person.

Brief is a short way to be fast

Many times we receive warning in our lives
Yet our minds are not always in a state of readiness!

If I knew how
I would abduct love and make it last.

Don't abuse happiness
It is some time a one time affair.

Happiness is a rare gem that we should Cherish!

A weak man is like a rubber band
He stretches the way he is pulled.

Being successful does not mean being above,
It means being one of the best.

Kindness out of duty is good for the receiver,
Kindness from the heart is good for the receiver
And rewarding for the giver.

Nothing cannot be defined, because nothing is none existent.

Life is a check written by God, an unlimited amount.

Love fades, but leaves some unknown ties that last forever.

A friend has the easiest chance to deceive, he's in.
An enemy is out, he has to get in,
That is to do what a friend can.

A sinners life is like a checking account,
A checking account you deposit, you withdraw, you use, its gone.
Life you live, You enjoy life, Life is over, You are done.

Sin is the tool Satan uses, To disconnect man from God.

Sin is a soul destroying Thief.
A Thief takes away your working properties.
Sin takes away your Intolerance. While sin is making you feel joy,
Satan is stealing your life.

Satan don't look like sin. With God in your heart, you can spot him.
Satan number one interest is the pulpit, He wants to stand men,
And tell all, what saith Satan.

If you buddy with Satan, he will follow all through life.

We can be an usher in life, Usher the last to the Church of God.

If we are being decent, We are respecting God.

Printed in the United States
By Bookmasters